A Gifted Child in Foster Care:
A Story of Resilience

STUDENT WORKBOOK
REVISED EDITION

READING COMPREHENSION & CHARACTER EDUCATION
for Students

Written by
Dr. Grace LaJoy Henderson

THE LESSONS IN THIS WORKBOOK UST BE USED IN CONJUNCTION WITH
THE NONFICTION BOOK ENTITLED, A GIFTED CHILD IN FOSTER CARE:
A STORY OF RESILIENCE - REVISED EDITION BY DR. GRACE LAJOY HENDERSON

Inspirations *by Grace LaJoy*
Post Office Box 181
Raymore, Missouri 64083

This workbook <u>must</u> be used in conjunction with the nonfiction book, **A Gifted Child in Foster Care:** *A Story of Resilience* – REVISED EDITION

A GIFTED CHILD IN FOSTER CARE - STUDENT WORKBOOK – REVISED EDITION
Copyright ©2010, 2020 Grace LaJoy Henderson
Published by Inspirations by Grace LaJoy
Raymore, Missouri

ISBN 978-1-7341868-1-9

All rights reserved. No portion of this book may be copied, reproduced or transmitted in any form without prior written permission from the publisher.

Printed in the United States of America

TABLE OF CONTENTS

Testimonials — vi

A Word from the Author — vii

Introduction — viii

Lesson One 1
- Main Idea and Supporting Details
- Sequencing
- Identifying Cause and Effect
- Interpreting and Evaluating Information
- Comparing and Contrasting
- Character Trait Discussion – *Appreciation*

Lesson Two 5
- Main Idea and Supporting Details
- Sequencing
- Identifying Cause and Effect
- Interpreting and Evaluating Information
- Comparing and Contrasting
- Character Trait Discussion - *Honesty*

Lesson Three 9
- Main Idea and Supporting Details
- Sequencing
- Identifying Cause and Effect
- Interpreting and Evaluating Information
- Character Trait Discussion - *Respect*

Lesson Four 11
- Main Idea and Supporting Details
- Sequencing
- Identifying Cause and Effect
- Interpreting and Evaluating Information
- Comparing and Contrasting
- Character Trait Discussion - *Dependable*

Lesson Five **15**

- Main Idea and Supporting Details
- Sequencing
- Identifying Cause and Effect
- Interpreting and Evaluating Information
- Comparing and Contrasting
- Character Trait Discussion - *Secure*
- Bonus Discussion

Lesson Six **19**

- Main Idea and Supporting Details
- Sequencing
- Identifying Cause and Effect
- Interpreting and Evaluating Information
- Comparing and Contrasting
- Character Trait Discussion - *Love*

Lesson Seven **23**

- Main Idea and Supporting Details
- Sequencing
- Identifying Cause and Effect
- Interpreting and Evaluating Information
- Comparing and Contrasting
- Character Trait Discussion - *Obedience*

Lesson Eight **27**

- Main Idea and Supporting Details
- Identifying Cause and Effect
- Interpreting and Evaluating Information
- Comparing and Contrasting
- Character Trait Discussion - *Content*

Lesson Nine **31**

- Main Idea and Supporting Details
- Sequencing
- Identifying Cause and Effect
- Comparing and Contrasting
- Character Trait Discussion - *Courage*

Lesson Ten **35**

- Main Idea and Supporting Details
- Sequencing
- Identifying Cause and Effect
- Interpreting and Evaluating Information
- Comparing and Contrasting
- Character Trait Discussion - *Encouragement*

Lesson Eleven **39**

- Main Idea and Supporting Details
- Sequencing
- Identifying Cause and Effect
- Interpreting and Evaluating Information
- Comparing and Contrasting
- Character Trait Discussion - *Diligence*

Lesson Twelve **43**

- Main Idea and Supporting Details
- Sequencing
- Identifying Cause and Effect
- Interpreting and Evaluating Information
- Comparing and Contrasting
- Character Trait Discussion - *Insight*

Lesson Thirteen **47**

- Interpreting and Evaluating Information
- Character Trait Discussion - *Forgiveness*

Lesson Fourteen **49**

- Interpreting and Evaluating Information
- Character Trait Discussion - *Building Self Esteem*

Bonus Character Trait Discussion – *Determination* **51**

Testimonials

"It's a new way to implement nonfiction, character education and key reading strategies."
~**Suzanne Wiley**, Reading Specialist - Lee's Summit R7 School District

"If taken to heart, the Character Trait Discussions in this workbook, will result in a more resilient child who can overcome adversity." ~**Dr. Steve McClure**, Assistant Director - University of Missouri, Kansas City - Charter School Center

"The lessons in this workbook help students understand the reading better. The discussion questions help students apply the character traits to their own life." ~**Shardae Williams**, 7th Grade Student - Smith Hale Middle School

"Several reading comprehension skills are reinforced in every lesson, which helps students learn. The character trait discussions help students apply life skills and make connections to the text."
~**Jennifer Gooding**, Reading Intervention Teacher - Belton School District

"…an excellent tool for students to learn. The reading comprehension skills coincide with the Department of Education's curriculum expectations." ~**Celest West**, Reading Teacher – Center Alternative School, Kansas City, MO

A Word from the Author

When I was two years old, my mother left me and my five brothers and sisters and she never came back! She left us with our father. As a single parent, Daddy did his best to raise us and tried very hard to keep us together. But when I was seven years old, he ended up leaving me and four of my brothers and sisters in a house alone. He took my oldest brother, who was fifteen years old at that time, with him. The oldest child left in the house was my fourteen-year-old brother.

Daddy had promised to send money and he even asked his girlfriend Rose and my Aunt Mattie to check on us. But somehow, the house we were left in ended up with no lights, no gas, no phone, no water, and no food. Even the lock on the front door was broken, leaving me feeling afraid.

One late night, at about two o'clock a.m., the sheriff came and removed us all from that house. "We are taking you to an emergency foster home for a nice hot breakfast, "the sheriff said to me. Since I had not had a good meal for several weeks, I was happy to go.

I lived in foster care for three years. I experienced numerous ups and downs while living in foster care, but one of the things that sticks with me is the fact that my school placed me, a foster child, in the Gifted and Talented class. I did not understand why I was chosen because I did not feel smart at all. I felt like my gifted classmates deserved to be in that class, but I did not.

Daddy finally met the state's requirement to take us home to live with him when I was ten years old. We were stable for about six months, then he began taking us with him as he traveled from state to state. He finally stopped taking us with him when I was twelve, and I began living with my eighteen-year-old sister.

I lived with my sister until I was eighteen years old, at which time I became a single parent and began living on my own. It was hard being a single parent. I worked and went to school while raising my two children. Today, my two children have grown up to be responsible adults. Both of them graduated from high school and went to college.

I have earned my Doctorate degree and I am the author of over thirty books including book, **A Gifted Child in Foster Care:** *A Story of Resilience*. In this book, I expound on my story of being abandoned by my mother and father. I share intimate details about my life experience before, during and after foster care. I also offer words of empowerment to children and parents. This book has already gained the attention of foster care and adoptive organizations as well as educators worldwide.

Sometimes I wonder what my life would have been like with a mother. But, if my life story would have been different, I would not be the person I am today, and I like who I am today!

Dr. Grace LaJoy, Author
A Gifted Child in Foster Care:
A Story of Resilience

Introduction

This workbook includes activities for every chapter of the *nonfiction* book "A Gifted Child in Foster Care: A Story of Resilience". You will read the book, alone or with a group. Then you will do the lessons from the workbook that coincides with each chapter.

The lesson activities will help you to:

- Develop a better understanding of what you have read.
- Identify and discuss positive character traits.

You will learn these Reading Comprehensive skills:

- Identifying the Main Idea and Supporting Details
- Sequencing Events
- Identifying Cause and Effect
- Comparing and Contrasting
- Interpreting and Evaluating Information
- Identifying and Discussing Character Traits

Reading Comprehension Skills

Identifying the Main Idea and Supporting Details

The main idea is the most important part of the chapter. It is the main thought that the author is trying to get across you. The rest of the chapter may contain details that support the main idea. The main idea may be found in any part of the chapter. More than one main idea may be found within a chapter.

Sequencing Events

Sequencing means to place information in a particular order. For example: Identifying what happened first, second, and third in the chapter.

Identifying Cause and Effect

Effect answers the question "What happened?" Cause answers the question "What made it happen?" or "Why did it happen?" Cause and effect may also include "Drawing Conclusions" or looking at something that has already happened and trying to figure out what is going to happen next.

Comparing and Contrasting

Comparing and contrasting means to identify what is the same and different about a person, place or thing. For example, two cars can be the same in some ways and different in others.

Interpreting and Evaluating Information

Interpreting and evaluating information includes reading a chapter and thinking carefully about what has been read. It also includes determining what is meant by the information in the chapter. You may examine information from a chart or a graph, then explain what it means.

Identifying and Discussing Character Traits

Identifying and discussing character traits include discovering virtues and attitudes of characters in the chapters. A Character Trait may be "respect". Identifying this trait may include discussing how "respect" is portrayed in a chapter. You may discuss how you would display "respect" towards yourself and others. The character trait discussion topics are designed to encourage you to advance to a higher level of critical thinking.

Lesson One

This lesson coincides with Chapter One of the book, A Gifted Child in Foster Care: A Story of Resilience
Chapter One – "Left by Mother"

Character Trait – "Appreciation"

Main Idea and Supporting Details

Place an "X" on the line beside the "main idea" of the story.

_____ Mother left when Grace was two years old and never came back.

_____ Grandmother believed Grace was a strong and resilient child.

_____ Grace stayed home with her mother while her father worked.

The <u>four</u> statements below "support" the main idea. Fill in the blanks with the correct word.

The words "your mother doesn't want you" _____ Grace.

Grace was _____ for her friends at school to know about her mother leaving.

Grace remembers both _____ and _____ things her mother.

Grace has gained a greater _____ for life because of her mother.

Sequencing

Place a "1" on the line beside the event that happened first in Chapter One.
Place a "2" on the line beside the event that happened second in Chapter One.
and so on...

____ Grace often wonders what type of life her mother is living

____ Grace's school mates asked, "Where is your mother?"

____ Grace feels a strong sense of love and loyalty towards her mother

____ Grace was born

____ Grace's mother left

____ Grace remembers a lot of things about her mother

A Guide to Reading and Comprehension & Character Education *for Students*
© Inspirations by Grace LaJoy

Identifying Cause and Effect

"Mother went out into the backyard one evening and lay down to hid in the tall, uncut grass because she feared being picked up by the state to be locked up again in a mental institution."

What is the cause? _____

What is the effect? _____

Interpreting and Evaluating Information

Circle all of the feelings Grace experienced after her mother left.

Devastation   Joy   Embarrassment   Fear   Guilt   Insecurity   Excitement   Rejection

Comparing and Contrasting

Name three(3) things that are different about these two stories from Chapter One

Mother made cookies	Mother popped popcorn
Example: Mother prepared cookies	Example: Mother prepared popcorn

Character Trait Discussion

The Character Trait for Lesson One is "Appreciation".

Appreciation means to feel "thankful".

Read the statement below. Then chose one of the questions below and answer it. Write your answer in the space provided then discuss it with your group.

Grace still loves and appreciates her mother even though she left her with her father and never came back.

1. Would you appreciate your mother if she left you and never came back? Why or why not?
2. Name a person who you appreciate. Why do you appreciate that person?
3. Why is it important to "appreciate" other people?

Lesson Two

This lesson coincides with Chapter Two of the book, A Gifted Child in Foster Care: A Story of Resilience
Chapter Two – "Living with Daddy"

Character Trait – "Honesty"

Main Idea and Supporting Details

Place an "X" on the line beside the "main idea" of the story.

_____ Daddy enjoyed the blues, love songs and gospel music.

_____ After Mother left, Daddy did all he could to care for his children.

_____ Daddy received help from Grace's Grandmother.

Write four "supporting details" for the main idea.

1. _____
2. _____
3. _____
4. _____

Sequencing

What did Daddy do <u>after</u> mother disappeared never to return?

_____

_____

_____

Identifying Cause and Effect

Grace believed her mother left because Daddy abused her.

What is the "Cause"? _____

What is the "Effect"? _____

Interpreting and Evaluating Information

What example did Grace write about, in Chapter Two, to show how determined she could be about a goal?

_____

_____

_____

Comparing and Contrasting

How was Daddy's treatment of Mother <u>different</u> from the way he treated the children.

_____

_____

_____

Character Trait Discussion

The Character Trait for Lesson Two is "Honesty"

Honesty means being truthful. Speaking the truth. Saying what is true.

Answer the <u>three</u> questions below. Write your answer in the spaces provided then discuss them with your group.

1. What was Grace's response when Daddy asked "Did you finish eating your cake?"
   _____

2. Was her response "honest"? Why or why not?

3. Describe a time when you were honest <u>or</u> *not* honest. What happened as a result?

_____

_____

_____

A Gifted Child in Foster Care – Student Workbook
© Inspirations by Grace LaJoy, LLC

Lesson Three

This lesson coincides with Chapter Three of the book, A Gifted Child in Foster Care: A Story of Resilience
Chapter Three – "Grandmother"

Character Trait – "Respect"

Main Idea and Supporting Details

Place an "X" on the line beside the "main idea" of the story.

_____ Daddy struggled to raise six children alone.

_____ Grace's first day of kindergarten was scary.

_____ Grandmother played an important role in Grace's life.

Write three "supporting details" for the main idea.

1. _____

2. _____

3. _____

Sequencing

Place a "1" on the line beside the event that happened first in Chapter Three
Place a "2" on the line beside the event that happened second in Chapter Three
and so on...

___ Grandmother enrolled Grace in School

___ Grace's mother disappeared

___ Daddy did not need Grandmother's assistance as much anymore

___ Grandmother adopted Grace's mother

___ Grandmother helped Daddy with Grace and her siblings

Identifying Cause and Effect

Entering the kindergarten class for the first time caused Grace to feel fearful.

What is the "Cause"? _____

What is the "Effect"? _____

Interpreting and Evaluating Information

Place a "T" on the line beside the statements that are "true" and an "F" on the ones that are false.

_____ Grandmother was an important influence in Grace's life

_____ Grandmother often disrespected Grace

_____ Grandmother instilled in Grace the love of learning

_____ Grandmother made everything a learning experience

Name three fears Grace had about remaining in her new kindergarten class without her grandmother there?

1. _____
2. _____
3. _____

Character Trait Discussion

The Character Trait for Lesson Three is "Respect"

Respect means showing kindness towards others regardless of their behavior. Having a positive attitude towards those who you like <u>and</u> those who you do not like.

Read the statement below. Then choose <u>one</u> of the questions below and answer it. Write your answer in the space provided then discuss it with your group.

Grandmother always showed "respect" towards Grace even when she misbehaved.

1. Name <u>three</u> ways Grandmother showed respect towards Grace.
2. Write about a time when someone showed "respect" towards you?
3. What are some ways we can "respect" each other.

_____
_____
_____
_____
_____

A Gifted Child in Foster Care – Student Workbook
© Inspirations by Grace LaJoy, LLC

Lesson Four

This lesson coincides with Chapter Four of the book, A Gifted Child in Foster Care: A Story of Resilience
Chapter Four – "Left by Father"

Character Trait – "Dependable"

Main Idea and Supporting Details

Place an "X" on the line beside the "main idea" of the story.

_____ Grandmother did not come to help after Father left.

_____ Grace's two brothers slept in shift in front of the front door.

_____ Daddy left Grace, her siblings in a house alone while he went to Florida for work.

Place an "X" on the line beside the "supporting details" that are true.

_____ Aunt Mattie brought some home-cooked food and quilts over.

_____ Rose came over ten times to check on the children.

_____ It appears Daddy sent money as he had promised.

_____ The money stopped but the lights, gas, water, and phone remained on.

Sequencing

Place a "1" on the line beside the event that happened first in Chapter Four
Place a "2" on the line beside the event that happened second in Chapter Four
Place a "3" on the line beside the event that happened second in Chapter Four

_____ Grace and her brothers and sisters were afraid.

_____ Daddy left the children in a house alone.

_____ The house the children were left in had no utilities and no phone.

Identifying Cause and Effect

Complete the sentence below with the correct answer.

Grace's father took her oldest brother with him when he left because…

_____

_____

_____

_____

_____

_____

Interpreting and Evaluating Information

Review Grace's Timeline on page 93 of A Gifted Child in Foster Care: A Story of Resilience and answer the following <u>two</u> questions.

1. What year did Grace's father leave the children in the house alone?

   _____

2. Was it was right for him to leave? Why or why not?

   _____

   _____

   _____

   _____

Comparing and Contrasting

What is the <u>difference</u> between why Mother left and why Father left?

Why did Mother leave?	Why did Father leave?

Did one parent leave the children in a safer situation than the other parent? Why or why not?

_____

_____

_____

Character Trait Discussion

The Character Trait for Lesson Four is "Dependable"

Dependable means being the type of person that others can count on. Being responsible. Keeping promises.

Answer the two questions below. Write your answers in the spaces provided then discuss them with your group.

1. Was Grace's father dependable? Why or why not?

   _____

   _____

   _____

   _____

   _____

   _____

   _____

   _____

2. Name three(3) ways that you can be dependable.

   1. _____

   2. _____

   3. _____

Lesson Five

This lesson coincides with Chapter Five of the book, A Gifted Child in Foster Care: A Story of Resilience
Chapter Five – "Living in Foster Care"

Character Trait – "Secure"

Main Idea and Supporting Details

Place an "X" on the line beside the "main idea" of the story.

_____ Foster care caused Grace to feel happy, safe and secure.

_____ Grandmother took care of Grace and her sister for a brief period of time.

_____ Grace did not understand why she was chosen for the Gifted and Talented program.

Write three "supporting details" for the main idea.

1. _____

2. _____

3. _____

Sequencing

Place a "1" on the line beside the event that happened first in Chapter Five
Place a "2" on the line beside the event that happened second in Chapter Five
and so on...

____ Grace lived with Big Mama.

____ Grace was placed in her school's Gifted and Talented program.

____ Father visited Big Mama's home.

____ The emergency foster lady cooked a large hot breakfast for the children.

____ The Sheriff took Grace and her brothers and sisters to an emergency foster home.

____ Grace lived with Grandmother.

Identifying Cause and Effect

What caused Grandmother to leave Grace and her sister sitting on the porch until the social worker came?

_____

_____

_____

Interpreting and Evaluating Information

Do you feel that it was right for Grandmother to leave Grace and her sister on the porch? Why or why not?

_____

_____

_____

_____

_____

Comparing and Contrasting

Name one difference between the emergency foster home and the home Grace was left in.

_____

_____

_____

Character Trait Discussion

The Character Trait for Lesson Five is "Secure".

Secure means feeling safe; not feeling fearful.

Read the five questions below. Then answer one of the questions. Write your answer in the space provided then discuss it with your group.

1. Did Grace feel "secure" in the home her father left her in? Why or why not?
2. Did Grace feel "secure" at the emergency foster home? Why or why not?
3. Did Grace feel "secure" living with Grandmother? Why or why not?
4. Did Grace feel "secure" living with Big Mama? Why or why not?

5. Did Grace feel "secure" in the Gifted and Talented classroom? Why or why not?

_____

_____

_____

_____

_____

_____

_____

_____

_____

_____

_____

_____

_____

_____

_____

_____

Bonus Discussion

Read the statement and answer the question below. Write your answer in the space provided then discuss it with your group.

Grace did not talk about how she felt about seeing her father after eighteen months. What feeling(s) do you think she felt? Why?

_____
_____
_____
_____
_____
_____
_____
_____
_____
_____
_____
_____
_____
_____
_____
_____

Lesson Six

This lesson coincides with Chapter Six of the book, A Gifted Child in Foster Care: A Story of Resilience
Chapter Six – "Separated From Siblings"

Character Trait – "Love"

Main Idea and Supporting Details

Place an "X" on the line beside the "main idea" of the story.

_____ Birth order played a big part in the way each child was effected by being separated.

_____ Terrance served in the United States Army.

_____ Grace was separated from all but one of her siblings during foster care.

Write three "supporting details" for the main idea.

1. _____

2. _____

3. _____

Sequencing

Name Grace's siblings from youngest to oldest.

1. _____

2. _____

3. _____

4. _____

5. _____

Identifying Cause and Effect

Read the following statement and answer the question below.

In Chapter Six Grace stated, "Excitement gripped me when I knew I was going to visit my siblings."

What caused Grace to feel excitement? _____

_____

Interpreting and Evaluating Information

Review Grace's Timeline on page 93 of A Gifted Child in Foster Care: A Story of Resilience and answer the following question:

What year did Grace begin living with Big Mama? _____

Name the sibling who also lived with Big Mama. _____

Write <u>three</u> things that Grace remembers about that sibling.

1. _____

2. _____

3. _____

Name the sibling who had the greatest influence on Grace. _____

Why was that sibling's influence so great? _____

_____

_____

Comparing and Contrasting

Choose <u>two</u> of Grace's siblings and write their names on the lines in the circles below. Now, name <u>two</u> ways the siblings are different and <u>one</u> way they are the same.

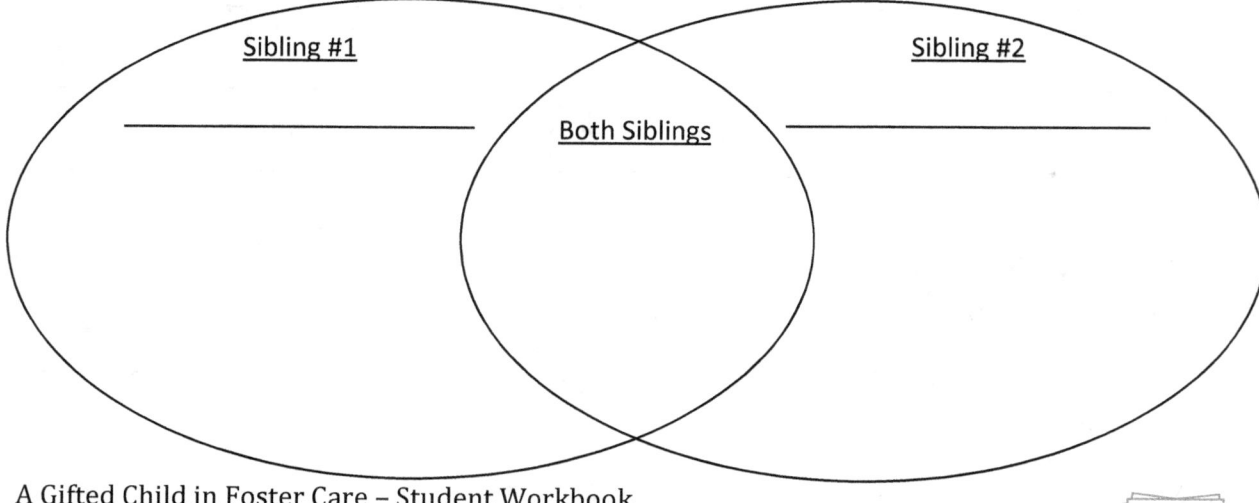

Character Trait Discussion

The Character Trait for Lesson Six is "Love"

Love means caring about someone, having kind thoughts about them, and appreciating the positive affect they have had on your life.

Answer the two questions below. Write your answers in the space provided then discuss them with your group.

Do you feel Grace loved her sisters and brothers? Why or why not?

_____

_____

_____

_____

_____

_____

_____

Name three things you can do to show someone you love them.

1. _____

2. _____

3. _____

Lesson Seven

This lesson coincides with Chapter Seven of the book, A Gifted Child in Foster Care: A Story of Resilience
Chapter Seven – "A Typical Day in Foster Care"

Character Trait – "Obedience"

Main Idea and Supporting Details

Place an "X" on the line beside the "main idea" of the story.

_____ Grace liked visiting the school library.

_____ Grace had a daily routine, which included various chores while living in foster care.

_____ If Big Mama was not happy, nobody was happy.

Write three "supporting details" for the main idea.

1. _____

2. _____

3. _____

Sequencing

A typical day in foster care included the nine activities below. What order did Grace do each activity listed below?

Place a "1" on the line next to the activity that Grace did first.
Place a "2" on the line next to the activity that Grace did second.
and so on…

_____ Took a bath   _____ Played outside

_____ Ate breakfast   _____ Walked to school

_____ Went to bed   _____ Completed chores

_____ Walked home from school   _____ Started on homework

_____ Ate dinner

Identifying Cause and Effect

Read the two questions below, then write the correct answer in the space provided.

1. What was the "effect" when Tina and Grace did not clean up correctly?

   _____

2. What caused Big Mama to have a bad mood?

   _____

   _____

Interpreting and Evaluating Information

Write three things that Grace liked most about school.

1. _____

2. _____

3. _____

Name one reason why Grace chose books that were easy to read when she went to the school library.

_____

_____

_____

_____

Comparing and Contrasting

Fill in the blanks below with the correct words.

Whereas Danisha was Grace's _____ sister, Tina was Grace's _____ sister.

Character Trait Discussion

The Character Trait for Lesson Seven is "Obedience"

Obedience means doing what your parent, teacher, or other authority figure instructs you to do. Doing the right thing.

Read the two instructions below. Write your answers to both in the space provided then discuss them with your group.

Name three ways Grace was obedient.

1. _____

2. _____

3. _____

Name three ways you can be obedient.

1. _____

2. _____

3. _____

Bonus Discussion

What are your thoughts about Big Mama telling Grace she could not eat breakfast anymore? Write your thoughts in the space below then discuss it with your group.

_____

_____

_____

_____

Lesson Eight

This lesson coincides with Chapter Eight of the book, A Gifted Child in Foster Care: A Story of Resilience
Chapter Eight – "How Foster Care Shaped My Life"

Character Trait – "Content"

Main Idea and Supporting Details

Place an "X" on the line beside the "main idea" of the story.

_____ Foster care met Grace's social, physical, mental and emotional needs.

_____ Big Mama took Grace to the drive-in.

_____ Grace has stability in her life today.

Write three "supporting details" for the main idea.

1. _____

2. _____

3. _____

Identifying Cause and Effect

Place an "X" on the line beside the correct answer.

What caused Grace to finally appreciate all the good things Big Mama did for her?

_____ She began to see how her time spent in foster care contributed to the stability she enjoys in her life today.

_____ She realized her children were thankful for Big Mama.

Interpreting and Evaluating Information

Unscramble the answers to the following question.

What <u>five</u> things did foster care offer Grace?

1. bsleat mheo rnotnenemiv

_____   _____   _____

2. lfmyia   iiistcavet

_____   _____

3. natoientt

_____

4. thhlae & tdlaen rcae

_____ & _____   _____

5. plseidnici

_____

Comparing and Contrasting

Name <u>three</u> differences between Grace's life *before* foster care and *during* foster care.

Before Foster Care	During Foster Care

Character Trait Discussion

The Character Trait for Lesson Eight is "Content"

Content means being happy with what you have and not worrying about what you don't have. Appreciating the good things in your life.

Answer <u>one</u> of the questions below. Write your answer in the space provided then discuss it with your group.

1. Was Grace "content" during foster care? Why or why not?
2. Are you "content"? Why or why not?
3. Name three things you could say to encourage someone who is not "content" with their life.

_____

_____

_____

_____

_____

_____

_____

_____

_____

_____

_____

_____

_____

_____

_____

_____

_____

Lesson Nine

This lesson coincides with Chapter Nine of the book, A Gifted Child in Foster Care: A Story of Resilience
Chapter Nine – "Life After Foster Care"

Character Trait – "Courage"

Main Idea and Supporting Details

Place an "X" on the line beside the "main idea" of the story.

_____ Grace got in more fights after foster care.

_____ Grace went to school with gangsters and children who carried weapons.

_____ Grace's father finally met the requirements to take her out of foster care.

Write three "supporting details" for the main idea.

1. _____

2. _____

3. _____

Sequencing

Place a "1" on the line next to the event that happened first.
Place a "2" on the line next to the event that happened second.
and so on…

_____ Grace met her father's girlfriend, Ms. Ruby.

_____ Grace's father took her to the three bedroom townhome where they would be living.

_____ Grace began sixth grade in North Carolina.

_____ Grace and her sisters rode the bus from Kansas City, Missouri to Charlotte, North Carolina.

_____ Grace's father moved them back and forth several times.

_____ Father met state requirements to get Grace out of foster care.

Identifying Cause and Effect

Place an "X" on the line beside the correct answer.

What caused Tracy to want to fight Grace?
_____ She wanted Grace to be a part of her gang.
_____ She believed Grace was taking all of her boyfriends.

Interpreting and Evaluating Information

Read the following question and write your answer on the line below.

What feeling do you think Grace felt while going to school with gangsters?

_____

Comparing and Contrasting

Read the following question and write your answer on the line below.

Why does Grace believe she got into fights *after* going to live with her father, but did not have fights *while* in foster care?

_____

_____

_____

_____

_____

Character Trait Discussion

The Character Trait for Lesson Nine is "Courage"

Courage means not being afraid. Being confident.

Answer one of the three questions below. Write your answer in the space provided then discuss it with your group.

1. Do you feel Grace had courage? Why or why not?
2. Describe a situation in which you displayed courage.
3. Describe a situation in which someone you know displayed courage.

Lesson Ten

This lesson coincides with Chapter Ten of the book, A Gifted Child in Foster Care: A Story of Resilience
Chapter Ten – "Daddy Left Again"

Character Trait – "Encouragement"

Main Idea and Supporting Details

Place an "X" on the line beside the "main idea" of the story.

_____ After Daddy got Grace out of foster care, he left again.

_____ Grace's life was threatened when she was thirteen years old.

_____ Daddy had good intentions and would never say anything to hurt Grace.

Write three "supporting details" for the main idea.

1. _____

2. _____

3. _____

Sequencing

Place a "1" on the line next to the event that happened first.
Place a "2" on the line next to the event that happened second.
and so on…

_____ Grace's teacher noticed her writing ability.

_____ Daddy left again.

_____ Grace realized she was not "hard-headed".

_____ Grace lived with Carla in a townhome.

Identifying Cause and Effect

Read the following question and write your answer in the space below.

What does Grace believe caused her grades to drop and to never again be recognized as a "gifted" student?

_____

_____

_____

_____

_____

_____

Interpreting and Evaluating Information

Review Grace's Timeline on page 93 of A Gifted Child in Foster Care: A Story of Resilience and answer the following question.

What year did Daddy leave Grace in North Carolina? _____

Comparing and Contrasting

Why did Daddy leave again?

_____

_____

Was Daddy's reason for leaving the second time the *same* or *different* from his reason for leaving the first time? (See Chapter Four for the reason Daddy left the first time)

_____

Character Trait Discussion

The Character Trait for Lesson Ten is "Encouragement"

Encouragement means saying or doing something to cause someone to believe they can be successful.

Answer <u>one</u> of the questions below. Write your answer in the space provided then discuss it with your group.

1. What did Grace's English teacher do to "encourage" her?
2. What did the high school principal say that made Grace feel encouraged?
3. Write three things you can say to encourage a friend or a classmate?

_____

_____

_____

_____

_____

_____

_____

_____

_____

_____

Lesson Eleven

This lesson coincides with Chapter Eleven of the book, A Gifted Child in Foster Care: A Story of Resilience
Chapter Eleven – "Pregnant at Seventeen"

Character Trait – "Diligence"

Main Idea and Supporting Details

Place an "X" on the line beside the "main idea" of the story.

_____ Grace used her creative writing talent.

_____ Kansas City is a great place for a teenage girl to live.

_____ Grace became a young mother of a baby girl.

Write three "supporting details" for the main idea.

1. _____

2. _____

3. _____

Sequencing

Place a "1" on the line next to the event that Grace did first.
Place a "2" on the line next to the event that Grace did second.
and so on...

_____ Began attending a local community college

_____ Won homecoming queen

_____ Became pregnant

_____ Gave birth to Arica

_____ Used her creative writing skills

_____ Began her senior year in Kansas City

Identifying Cause and Effect
Read the following question and write your answer in the space below.

What *caused* Grace to leave her first apartment with her baby?

_____

_____

_____

_____

Interpreting and Evaluating Information

Grace became a mother at age eighteen.

Using the glossary on pages 97-99 of A Gifted Child in Foster Care: A Story of Resilience, write the definition for the word "mother" in the space below.

_____

_____

_____

Comparing and Contrasting
Fill in the blanks below with the correct words.

Whereas Grace attended school in _____ _____ in

the eleventh grade, she attended school in _____ _____

during her last year of high school.

Character Trait Discussion
The Character Trait for Lesson Eleven is "Diligence"

Diligence means to keep trying to be successful even when things are hard. Overcoming an obstacle or a challenge.

Answer <u>one</u> of the four questions below. Write your answer in the space provided then discuss it with your group.

1. In what way was Grace diligent?
2. How did Grace's diligence affect her children?
3. Name an obstacle or challenge that you have overcome? What did you do to overcome it?
4. Name a person you know who has been diligent. What did that person do to overcome their obstacle or challenge?

_____

_____

_____

_____

_____

_____

_____

_____

_____

_____

_____

_____

_____

_____

Lesson Twelve

This lesson coincides with Chapter Twelve of the book, A Gifted Child in Foster Care: A Story of Resilience **Chapter Twelve – "My Gift Revealed"**

Character Trait – "Insight"

Main Idea and Supporting Details

Place an "X" on the line beside the "main idea" of the story.

_____ Grace was abandoned by her mother and her father

_____ Grace's realized writing was her gift and began to use it.

_____ Grace volunteered as Youth Department Director.

Write three "supporting details" for the main idea.

1. _____
2. _____
3. _____

Sequencing

Place a "1" on the line next to the event that happened first in Chapter Twelve.
Place a "2" on the line next to the event that happened second in Chapter Twelve.
and so on...

_____ Grace published her fist book of poetry

_____ Grace often wondered what her gift was

_____ Grace helped other writers to become authors

_____ Grace volunteered as Youth Drama Director

Identifying Cause and Effect

Read the following question. Write your answer in the space below.

What caused Grace to be shaped into the person she is today?

_____

_____

_____

_____

Interpreting and Evaluating Information
Fill in the blanks with the correct words.

The _____ while in foster care instilled the discipline Grace needs today to create her _____, accomplish her _____, and fulfill her _____.

Comparing and Contrasting
Answer the following question in the space provided below.

How is Grace's life different now than it would have been if her story had been different.

_____

_____

_____

Character Trait Discussion
The Character Trait for Lesson Twelve is "Insight"

Insight means seeing something good in the midst of a bad situation. Seeing something positive about a person that the person does not see yet.

Answer one of the questions below. Write your answer in the space provided then discuss it with your group.

1. What insight did Grace gain from other people about her gift?
2. What insight did Grace gain as a result of being chosen for the gifted and talented program?
3. Describe a time when you, or someone you know, saw something good in the midst of a bad situation.

_____

Lesson Thirteen

This lesson coincides with Chapter Thirteen of the book, A Gifted Child in Foster Care: A Story of Resilience **Chapter Thirteen – "Empowerment for Children"**

Character Trait – "Forgiveness"

Interpreting and Evaluating Information

Read the two questions below and place and "X" on the line next to the correct answer.

1. What did Grace have to let go of in order to walk into her successful future?

    _____ Her best friend
    _____ Her painful past
    _____ Her dog

2. How long did Grace dwell on the negative, hurtful things after she left foster care?

    _____ Five months
    _____ Thirty years
    _____ Ten years

Circle all of the correct responses.

What positive things did Grace dwell on that caused her to truly let go of the negative experiences?

Stable home environment	Being "smart" or "gifted"
Her beauty	Having a brand new bike
Good physical hygiene	Being an unwed mother
Going to church	Learning to cook
Proper housekeeping	Regular health care

Fill in the blanks below with the correct words.

1. The best way to start moving _____ is to

    _____ from looking back.

2. If used effectively, your life experiences will make you _____

    and _____ others.

True or False
Write a "T" on the line next to the statement below if it is true and an "F" if it is false.

_____ Three things you can do to use your life experiences effectively are: Recognize your power, be confident, and take advantage of opportunities.

_____ You were born for a purpose and you should never give up.

Character Trait Discussion
The Character Trait for Lesson Thirteen is "Forgiveness"

Forgiveness to let go of negative past experiences and move forward. To release someone of something they did to hurt you. To show love toward someone who has done something wrong.

Chose one of the three questions below. Write your answer in the space provided then discuss it with your group.

1. What caused forgiveness to be released in Grace's heart? Who did she have to forgive?

2. Think of someone who hurt you. Have you forgiven that person? If so, how were you able to do it? If not, why not?

3. Do you feel forgiveness is important? Why or why not?

_____

_____

_____

_____

_____

_____

_____

_____

Lesson Fourteen

This lesson coincides with Chapter Fourteen of the book, A Gifted Child in Foster Care: A Story of Resilience **Chapter Fourteen – "Empowerment for Parents"**

Character Trait – "Building Self-esteem"

Interpreting and Evaluating Information

Read the question below and place and "X" on the line next to the correct answer.

1. What is a "gift"?

    _____ A birthday present

    _____ Doing something nice for someone

    _____ An unlearned talent

Circle all of the correct responses.

Which of the following steps will help parents empower their child?

    Buying their child a pet

    Paying attention to what their child enjoys

    Recognizing what their child is naturally good at

    Giving their child money

    Knowing that they have the power to shape their child's life

Fill in the blanks below with the correct words.

1. All children are _____ in one way or another.
2. One who has a gift _____ using it.

True or False
Write a "T" on the line next to the statement below if it is true and an "F" if it is false.

_____ Parents should provide opportunities for their child to participate in the thing he/she enjoys.

_____ You should not pursue your gift unless it will cause you to make a lot of money.

Character Trait Discussion
The Character Trait for Lesson Fourteen is "Building Self-esteem"

Building Self-esteem means doing or saying something to empower someone to know that they are important. Assuring someone that they have the power to do great things.

Chose one of the three questions below. Write your answer in the space provided then discuss it with your group.

1. Parents can build their children's self esteem by helping them to recognize that they have a gift. Can you think of other ways parents can help build children's self-esteem?

2. What are two things your teacher can say or do to help build your self-esteem?

3. What are three things you can do or say to help build someone else's self-esteem?

_____
_____
_____
_____
_____
_____
_____
_____
_____
_____
_____
_____
_____
_____
_____

A Gifted Child in Foster Care – Student Workbook
© Inspirations by Grace LaJoy, LLC

Bonus Character Trait Discussion

The Bonus Character Trait is "Determination"

Determination means refusing to give up regardless of obstacles. Doing everything in your power to complete a task.

Choose one of the three questions below and answer it. Write your answer in the space provided then discuss it with your group.

1. Have you ever had determination to achieve a goal?
   If yes, write that goal below and explain how you achieved it.
2. What future goals have you made for yourself? How do you plan to achieve them?
3. Do you feel "determination" is important? Why or why not?

_____

_____

_____

_____

_____

_____

_____

_____

_____

_____

_____

_____

_____

_____

A Gifted Child in Foster Care: *A Story of Resilience*
BOOK – ISBN: 978-1-7341868-0-2
REVISED EDITION

A great reading source for teachers, counselors and students. It is a true story of hope, determination, and overcoming adversity.

In this book, Dr. Grace LaJoy shares her life story of being deserted by her mother, living in foster care, and ending up in a gifted and talented class while still in foster care.

A Gifted Child in Foster Care: *A Story of Resilience*
STUDENT WORKBOOK – ISBN: 978-1-7341868-1-9
REVISED EDITION

The lessons in this workbook will improve reading comprehension for students, while changing attitudes and building character.

Students will read the chapters in the nonfiction book, A Gifted Child in Foster Care: A Story of Resilience, individually or as a group. Then they will do the lessons from this workbook that coincides with each chapter.

A Gifted Child in Foster Care: *A Story of Resilience*
TEACHER'S GUIDE – ISBN: 978-1-7341868-2-6
REVISED EDITION

This workbook for students will assist teachers in fulfilling the state requirements of the Grade-Level Expectations for Communication/Language Arts.

Teachers will be able to lead students in critical thinking exercises. Students will be able to develop and apply skills and strategies to comprehend, analyze and evaluate nonfiction.

The Teacher's Guide contains the answers to the lesson activities in the Student Workbook.

When Grace LaJoy originally published her foster care story, *A Gifted Child in Foster Care*, she thought she would *never* find her mother. But, she found her after 49 years! Now she is sharing her fascinating journey in an inspiring series you will love!

Titles include:
Finding Mother after Five Decades: *A Story of Hope*
Reuniting with Mother: *A Story of Tenacity*
After the Reunion: *A Story of Acceptance*
Diary of Emotions: *Thoughts and Feelings*

Discussion Questions in the back of each book are designed to increase awareness and discussion about mental health.

Questions Teachers Can Ask aid in increasing reading comprehension skills in the classroom.

This inspiring series offers hope to anyone searching for a lost loved one. You enjoyed Grace LaJoy's foster care story. Now, collect the entire Finding Mother Series today!

Available in softcover and Kindle eBook
Collect them all at Amazon.com
www.gracelajoy.com

Finding Mother after Five Decades: A Story of Hope
Grace LaJoy's determination pays off when she finally finds her mother who abandoned her at age two. Discover the specific details of her intriguing journey in *Finding Mother after Five Decades*, BOOK 1 of the Finding Mother Series

Reuniting with Mother: A Story of Tenacity
What happens when Grace LaJoy and her siblings come face-to-face with their estranged mother after 49 years? How does she receive them? Find out in *Reuniting with Mother*, BOOK 2 of the Finding Mother Series

After the Reunion: A Story of Acceptance
After a very emotional reunion, Grace LaJoy has two concerns to address with her long-lost mother. What are her concerns? Does she get the answers she needs from her mother? Find out in *After the Reunion*, BOOK 3 of the Finding Mother Series

Diary of Emotion: Thoughts and Feelings
After reuniting with her mother after 49 years, Grace LaJoy toils with an array of thoughts and feeling. She reveals them all in *Diary of Emotions*, BOOK 4 of the Finding Mother Series

www.ingramcontent.com/pod-product-compliance
Lightning Source LLC
Chambersburg PA
CBHW051423070526
44584CB00023B/3556